Brass

Wendy Lynch

Customer Service 888-454-2279
Visit our website at www.heinemannraintree.com

Designed by Joanna Hinton-Malivoire and John Walker
Printed in China by South China Printing Company

10 09 08 07 06
10 9 8 7 6 5 4 3 2 1

New edition ISBN: 1-4034-8864-9 (hardcover)
                     1-4034-8870-3 (paperback)

The Library of Congress has cataloged the first edition as follows:
Lynch, Wendy, 1945-
     Brass / Wendy Lynch.
          p. cm. -- (Musical Instruments)
     Includes bibliographical references (p.) and index.
     ISBN 1-58810-233-5
     1. Brass instruments--Juvenile literature. [1. Brass instruments.] I.
Title. II. Series.

ML933 .L96 2001
788.9'19--dc21
                              2001002882

Acknowledgments
The publishers would like to thank the following for permission to reproduce photographs: Alamy/ David Sanger Photography, p. 16; Corbis, pp. 14, 20, 22, 24; Gareth Boden, pp. 28, 29; Photodisc, pp. 6, 7, 10; Photo edit/ Tony Freeman, p. 8; Photofusion, p. 9 (Ray Roberts); Pictor, pp. 4, 19, 23; Redferns, pp. 11 (Odile Noel), 15 (Odile Noel), 27 (Paul Massey); Rex Features, pp. 21 (Denis Cameron), p. 25; Robert Harding, p. 17; Stone, pp. 5, 26; The Stock Market p. 12; Travel Ink (Derek Allan), p. 18.

Cover photograph reproduced with permission of Getty Images/ Taxi.

The publishers would like to thank Nancy Harris for her assistance in the preparation of this book.

Every effort has been made to contact copyright holders of any material reproduced in this book. Any omissions will be rectified in subsequent printings if notice is given to the publisher.

The paper used to print this book comes from sustainable sources.

Any words appearing in the text in bold, **like this**, are explained in the Glossary.

Contents

Making Music Together

There are many musical instruments in the world. Each instrument makes a different sound. We can make music together by playing these instruments in a band or an **orchestra**. An orchestra is a large group of musicians.

Bands and orchestras are made up
of different groups of instruments.

One of these groups is called brass.
You can see brass instruments in this
marching band.

What Are Brass Instruments?

Brass instruments are often made of brass. Brass is a strong metal. It does not **rust**. Brass instruments can be made out of other metals. Some are made of wood. Some are made of horn or shell.

tuba

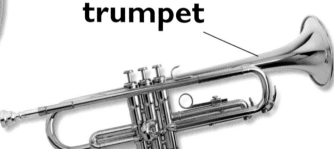

trumpet

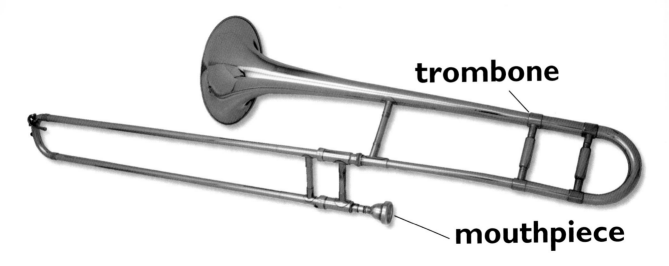

trombone

mouthpiece

Brass instruments make sounds. To make a sound you press your lips against the **mouthpiece**. You then blow air into it. The movement of your lips helps to make the sound.

French horn

bugle

The Trumpet

The trumpet is a brass instrument. You can learn to play the trumpet with a teacher. You can play the trumpet alone. This is called playing **solo**.

You can play the trumpet with other instruments. You can play it with a trombone. You can play it in a group. You can play it in a band. You can play it in an **orchestra**.

Making a Noise

The trumpet is a long, thin metal tube. It is **coiled**. It has a **mouthpiece**.

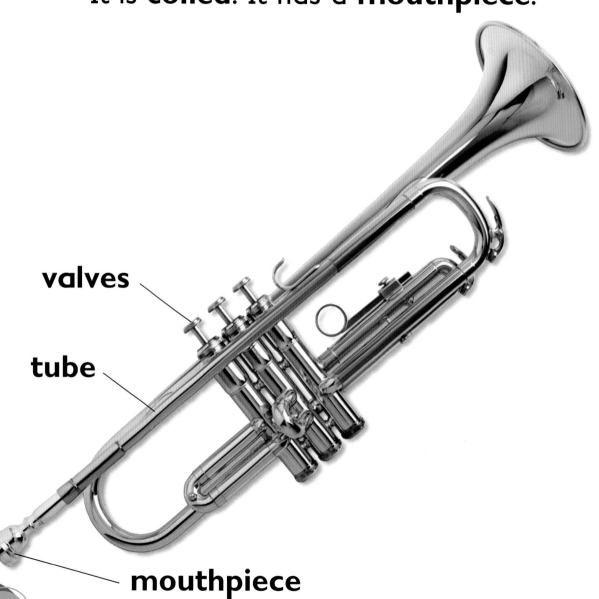

valves

tube

mouthpiece

When you blow into the mouthpiece it moves the air inside the tube. The air moves quickly from side to side.

Changing the Sound

You also press the valves with your fingers. This changes the sound.

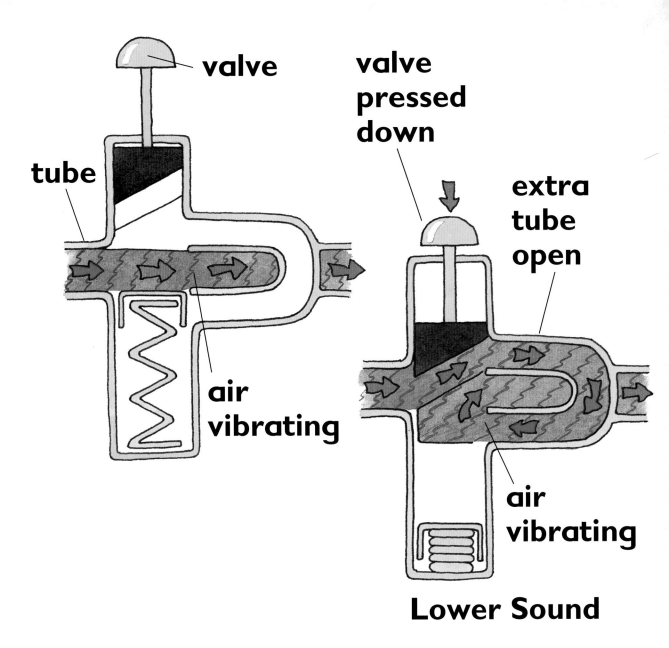

valve

valve
pressed
down

tube

extra
tube
open

air
vibrating

air
vibrating

Lower Sound

This makes the air **vibrate** more slowly.
This makes the sound lower.

The Cornet and the Trombone

The cornet is like a trumpet but smaller. You can sometimes hear the cornet playing **solo** in a band. It has a sweet sound. You can often hear the cornet in **jazz** music. Jazz is an old style of music that is often made up as it is played.

You play the trombone in a different way than other brass instruments. The trombone has a slide. The player moves the slide in and out to change the notes.

Big Brass

The tuba is a large brass instrument. It has a rich, low sound. It takes a lot of breath to play the tuba. This is because it is so big.

This is a sousaphone. The sousaphone is usually played standing up. The player must stand inside the tube of the instrument.

Marching Band

In a marching band, you can hear brass, and other instruments. All the players play their musical instruments as they march. They read music from cards clipped onto the instrument.

Marching bands often lead parades through towns and cities. They march on special days of celebration.

The Wider Family

The bugle is a small copper horn. You can only play a few notes on the bugle. Long ago, the bugle was used to send signals to soldiers at war. Different sounds had different meanings.

The conch trumpet is made from a shell. It is a brass instrument. This is because you play it by buzzing your lips into the **mouthpiece**.

Around the World

You can find brass instruments all over the world. The dung chen comes from Tibet. You can hear this trumpet in a **Buddhist temple**.

dung chen

This is a didgeridoo. It comes from Australia. It is made from the branch of a tree.

Famous Musicians and Composers

Haydn was a famous **composer**. A composer is a person who writes music. He wrote a trumpet **concerto**. A concerto is a piece of music in three parts.

Wynton Marsalis is a famous musician.
He plays the trumpet.

New Music

Today you can also hear brass instruments in **soul**, **rock**, and **pop bands**. This band is playing soul music.

A **synthesizer** is a keyboard. It can make many different sounds. It can make the sounds of all the brass instruments.

Sound Activity

- You can feel what it is like to play a brass instrument.

- Close your lips together tightly.

- Now blow against your fingers until you make a noise.

- Can you feel your lips **vibrating**?

28

- Roll a sheet of paper into the shape of a cone.

- Buzz your lips into the small end.

- To make a different sound place your hand against the large end of the cone.

Thinking About Brass

You can find the answers to all of these questions in this book.

1. Why is brass good for making musical instruments?
2. What is a valve on a brass instrument for?
3. Which brass instrument do you need to stand inside to play?
4. Where can you hear a dung chen?

More Books to Read

Knight, M. J. *Brass and Woodwind: Musical Instruments of the World.* Mankato, Minn: Smart Apple Media, 2005.

Pipe, Jim. *How Does a Trumpet Work?* New York: Franklin Watts Ltd, 2002.

Glossary

Buddhist temple special building where people who believe in Buddhism go to pray

coiled something curled or wound into a ring

composer person who writes music

concerto piece of music in three parts, often for one instrument and an orchestra You say *con-cher-toe*

jazz old style of music from the United States that is often made up as it is played

mouthpiece part of the instrument placed in or near the mouth

orchestra large group of musicians who play their musical instruments together You say *or-kes-tra*

pop band group of musicians who play music of the last 50 years. A lot of people like this music.

rock band group of musicians who play a type of pop music with a strong beat

rust brown or red coating that forms on some metals when they get wet

solo song or piece of music for one person

soul band group of musicians who play a kind of pop music that is full of feeling. Brass instruments are often played by soul bands.

synthesizer electronic instrument that can make or change many different sounds You say *sintha-size-er*

vibrate move up and down or from side to side very quickly

Index